It's My Body

Neck and Shoulders

Lola Schaefer

www.raintreepublishers.co.uk
Visit our website to find out more information about **Raintree** books.

To order:
☎ Phone 44 (0) 1865 888112
📄 Send a fax to 44 (0) 1865 314091
💻 Visit the Raintree Bookshop at **www.raintreepublishers.co.uk** to browse our catalogue and order online.

First published in Great Britain by Raintree, Halley Court, Jordan Hill, Oxford OX2 8EJ, part of Harcourt Education.
Raintree is a registered trademark of Harcourt Education Ltd.

Editorial: Jennifer Gillis and Diyan Leake
Design: Sue Emerson and Michelle Lisseter
Picture Research: Jennifer Gillis
Production: Lorraine Hicks

Originated by Dot Gradations
Printed and bound in China by South China Printing Company

ISBN 1 844 21651 9
07 06 05 04 03
10 9 8 7 6 5 4 3 2 1

British Library Cataloguing in Publication Data
Schaefer, Lola
Neck and shoulders
612.9'3
A full catalogue record for this book is available from the British Library.

Acknowledgements
The publishers would like to thank the following for permission to reproduce photographs: Corbis pp. 4 (George Shelley), 15 (Alan Jakubek), 16 (Ken Kaminesky), 20 (Tom & Dee Ann McCarthy); Custom Medical Stock Photo p. 23; Getty Images p. 9B (Chris Cole/All Sport); Heinemann Library pp. 5 (Brian Warling), 6 (Brian Warling), 7 (Robert Lifson), 8 (Brian Warling), 9T (Brian Warling), 14 (Brian Warling), 17 (Brian Warling), 21 (Brian Warling), 22 (Brian Warling), back cover (throat, shoulder, Brian Warling); PhotoEdit p. 13 (Jeff Greenberg); PhotoTake pp. 10 (Benedet), 18 (CNRI); PictureQuest p. 12 (Bob Daemmrich/Stock Boston, Inc.).

Cover photograph reproduced with permission of Photonica (Lisa Pines).

Some words are shown in bold, **like this**. You can find them in the glossary on page 23.

Contents

What are my neck and shoulders?

Your neck and shoulders are parts of your body.

Your body is made up of many parts.

Your neck and shoulders join other parts of your body.

They help you move your head and move your arms.

Where is my neck?

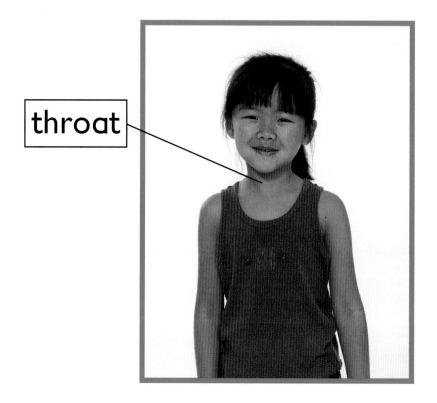

throat

Your neck is at the top of your body.

The front of your neck is called your throat.

neck

Your neck helps your head move.

You can move your head from side to side and up and down.

What does my neck look like?

Your neck is covered with smooth skin.

Some necks are thin.

Other necks are thick.

What is inside my neck?

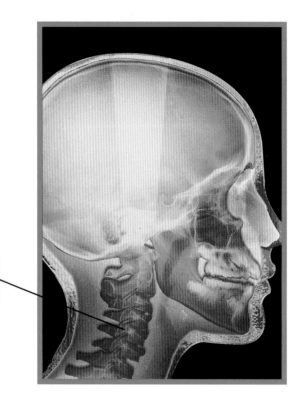

neck

There are **muscles** and **bones** inside your neck.

You use muscles to move your bones.

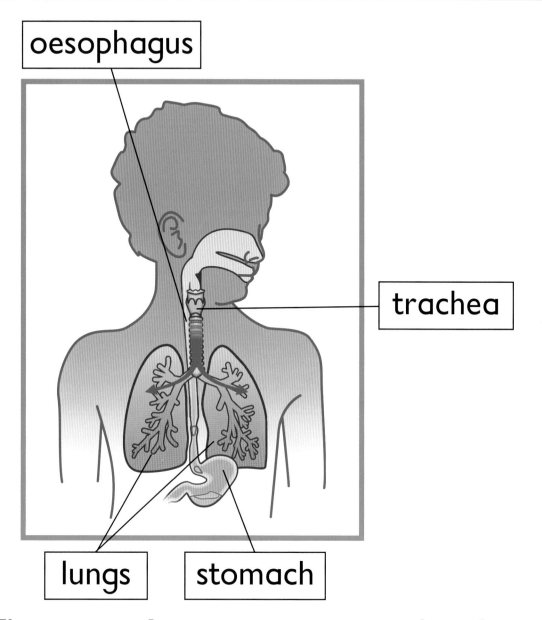

oesophagus

trachea

lungs

stomach

The **oesophagus** in your neck takes food to your **stomach**.

The **trachea** takes air to your **lungs**.

What can I do with my neck?

You use your neck to turn your head left and right.

You use it to nod your head.

You can bend your neck back to look up at the sky.

You can bend it to look down at your feet.

Where are my shoulders?

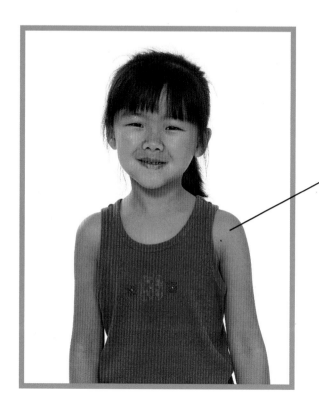

shoulder

Your shoulders are at the tops of your arms.

You have two shoulders.

Shoulders are where your arms join your body.

Shoulder **joints** help your arms move.

What do my shoulders look like?

Shoulders are covered with smooth skin.

Grown-ups have big shoulders.

Babies have little shoulders.

What is inside my shoulders?

shoulder bone

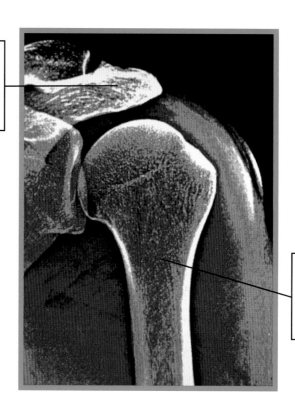

arm bone

There are **bones** inside your shoulders.

The arm bone fits in the shoulder bone.

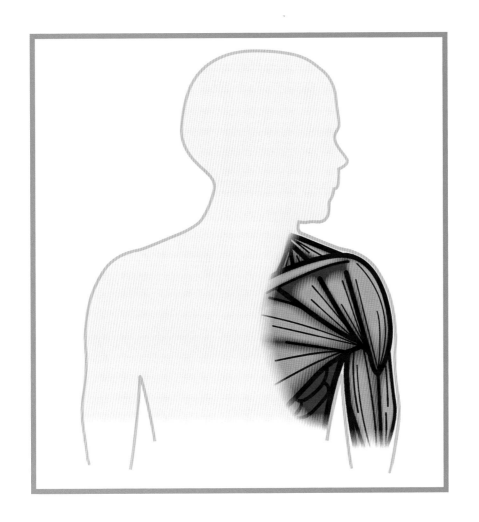

There are **muscles** inside your shoulders.

You use your muscles to move your bones.

What can I do with my shoulders?

You can use your shoulders to move your arms up high.

When you shrug your shoulders, it means that you don't know.

Quiz

Do you know what these are?

Look for the answers on page 24.

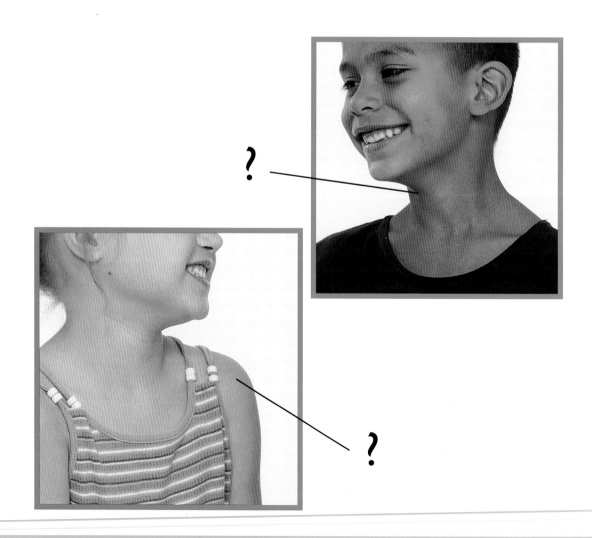

?

?

Glossary

bone
hard part inside your body

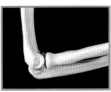
joint
a part of your body where bones come together so they can move

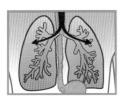
lungs
the parts inside you where the air goes when you breathe

muscle
a part in your body that you use to move with

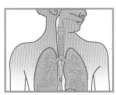
oesophagus
(uh-SOF-uh-gus) the part inside your body that takes the food down to your stomach

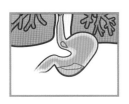
stomach
the part inside your body where the food goes

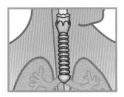
trachea
(tra-KEE-yuh) the part inside your throat where the air goes down into your lungs

Index

Answers to quiz on page 22

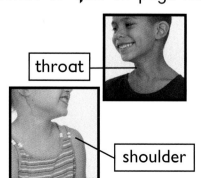

throat

shoulder

24

Titles in the It's My Body series include:

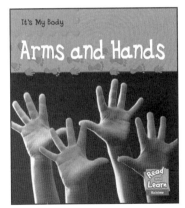

Hardback   1 844 21647 0

Hardback   1 844 21648 9

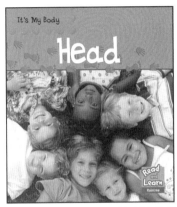

Hardback   1 844 21649 7

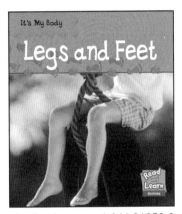

Hardback   1 844 21650 0

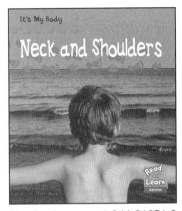

Hardback   1 844 21651 9

Find out about the other titles in this series on our website www.raintreepublishers.co.uk